Smokes

by Andrew Jefford

with

Reginald Whiff

Illustrated by
Satoshi Kambayashi

In memory of Clarissa Overend, 1931-1995:
Les belles d'autrefois ont fermé leurs paupières

First published in Great Britain in 1996 by
EVENING STANDARD BOOKS
Northcliffe House, 2 Derry Street, London W8 5EE

ISBN 1 900625 35 0

Publishing Manager Joanne Bowlby
Editorial Manager Charlotte Coleman-Smith
Production Manager Roger Hall
Index by Karin Woodruff

Designed by Nick Cave
With thanks to Sally Blackmore

A CIP catalogue record for this book is available from the British Library.

Printed and bound in Italy by Vallardi Industrie Grafiche, Milan.

This book may be ordered by post direct from the publisher,
but please try your bookshop first.

Contents

Introduction

In the autumn of 1994, the editor of *ES* Magazine, Adam Edwards, decided that it was time to launch a 'Smokes' column. Drinkers are well-served by newspapers; smokers less so. I, a committed though furtive cigar and pipe-user, was one of the writers drafted in to assist with the task. Shortly after this, by an extraordinary stroke of good fortune, I met, one balmy afternoon in Green Park, Mr Reginald Whiff.

I had, so far as I recall, just been to a wine tasting at one of the embassies in Belgrave Square, and I had an hour or so to dissipate before attending a further tasting in John Adam Street, near Charing Cross. I decided to sit in what remained of the day's sunshine and work a little at drafts in hand for 'Smokes'. One of these concerned clay pipes. After a while, I became conscious of a tall person to my right releasing a quantity of aromatic pipe smoke into the golden sunbeams. I looked up, and was astonished to see an elderly man with a neatly trimmed moustache smoking, with the serenity of an infant at his mother's breast, a clay churchwarden pipe. I gazed at him, open-mouthed.

'Does my smoke discomfit you?' he enquired, in tones I had only previously heard on those occasions when the *Evening Standard*'s art critic shimmered through the office. I assured him that it did the opposite; that, indeed, he could have been engaged in no activity more fascinating to me at that moment. I explained; he discoursed;

and a friendship from which I have been overwhelmingly the beneficiary began. So who is Whiff? I wish I was able to answer that question satisfactorily, but those biographical details which I have been able to piece together are sadly fragmentary. Nonetheless I will tell you what I know.

Reginald Whiff was born sometime during the 1920s. The Whiffs hailed from Sutherland (Whiff Manse, a mournful fortress long ruined, is to be found just to the west of Scourie, though Whiff himself has never acknowledged its existence); young Reginald seems to have been brought up in colonial surroundings in Hyderabad. He travelled much in his youth, and his wartime experiences, unquestionably formative, were spent in work of the highest danger and secrecy. I estimate that these covert and mobile activities lasted perhaps fifteen years after the War; but I am at a loss to say exactly what Whiff has been engaged in, in a professional sense, since 1960 or so. Perhaps a little 'consultancy' in the areas with which he was already familiar? All I have been able to detect, at any rate, is a gentle decline into relative indigence, shadowed by the steady contraction of a once-glorious social circle. His closest living friend is Mr Bertram 'Buffy' Wigg-Pitt, who now lives in a nursing home in Hampshire, and from whom, during one short and surreal visit, I have obtained most of these biographical details.

Whiff never married; I have, however, learned of a number of liaisons with, among others, a Balkan princess, an American heiress named Stumpp, and a Moroccan *danseuse*; regular readers will already know that the love of Whiff's life appears to have been the noted society beauty Clarissa Overend née Willoughby-Glossop, who predeceased her indulgent and reclusive husband Jasper Overend (the distinguished taxidermist and philanthropist) in 1995. Whiff has a nephew, Roddy, who has worked in an obscure capacity for several motor-racing teams, and whose existence naturally suggests that Whiff has a sibling. Roddy, however, is strangely reluctant to talk about his parents, and Buffy Wigg-Pitt simply laughed and nudged me repeatedly in a disarming manner when I asked about Whiff's brother or sister. Perhaps the connection is one, primarily, of affection.

Whiff lives in rooms in Pall Mall, 'done' by the faithful Gloria Sludgett and owned by Mr Harry Whipper of Croydon. He maintains a remarkable friendship with his former accountant Kym de Wynter, a plump Gay Rights activist whose multiple facial rings (eyebrow, nose, lip and, more mundanely, ears) never fail to attract comment. This friendship demonstrates Whiff's remarkable openness and curiosity about a world in which he seems to play so anachronistic a role.

For he is, above all, a smoker. To say that he lives to smoke is to do no more than state the obvious. He is a voracious consumer of cigarettes (especially untipped traditional brands such as Player's, purest Virginias like Davidoff Magnums, French *tabacs bruns* and, when he can get them, Turkish and Oriental brands) at various snatched moments during the day. For serious smoking (that is to say for periods of half-an-hour or more) he favours cigars and pipe tobacco. I have been able to prevail upon him to try various cigars for the purposes of the 'Smokes' column in *ES* Magazine, but in truth he remains deeply wedded to his beloved Havanas. In his pipe smoking, however, he is extremely catholic; not only does he own a huge variety of pipes, but he also possesses a remarkable 'tobacco library' assembled over many years and including many long-discontinued brands. His knowledge of matters fumatory is remarkable.

The column could not, indeed, be written without Whiff. The stamp of his scholarship lies upon every one of these pieces, even those for which his help is not (generally at his own modest insistence) openly acknowledged. I am happy to make this clear at the outset. Times, of course, are not now easy for the smoker of absolute dedication and commitment. Nonetheless Whiff has managed, with some of the remarkable mental flexibility he shows at every turn, to accommodate himself to the changing temper of an increasingly smoke-free age. He always disdained the notion that he might be addicted to tobacco, so his spending time in 'smoke-free zones' gives him, he claims, 'the agreeable opportunity of demonstrating my equanimity at abstention'. Perhaps so. He is, by contrast, a fierce defender of the private realm, of an individual's right to engage in whatever activities he or she might choose within the four walls of a private address; hence, I suspect, his sympathy with many of the battles fought by Kym de Wynter. Most of his smoking is now done at home — and, of course, when the weather permits (as it did so memorably on that first occasion) outdoors.

His health, I am happy to report, despite what must be recognised as a lifetime's pulmonary abuse, remains good; his carriage is upright; his temper, in the face of whatever the future may hold, serene.

Andrew Jefford
Sevenoaks, Kent

Foreword

My young friend Jefford has asked me to write a short foreword to this collection of 'Smokes' columns, and I am happy to oblige.

I was born into a world which smoked. I will, before too long, die out of one which does not smoke. Three centuries of rich nicotian culture will come to an end. Perhaps not totally (there will surely be a permanent future for fine cigars), yet most will smoke only very occasionally or not at all. The loss of a culture which has brought great pleasure and solace to many should not be contemplated lightly. If we are able, with these little 'puffs' of text, to salvage some of that culture from the coming darkness, we will not have worked in vain.

I don't have anything else to say, other than that almost all of the so-called biographical information provided by Jefford in his Introduction is without any factual basis whatsoever. Buffy Wigg-Pitt is a terrible fabricator and tease, and Jefford should have known better than to believe everything he was told by a near-senile gamesman in a nursing home. (Sorry, Buffy!).

Reginald Whiff

Reginald Whiff
Pall Mall, London

1: Puffs from the past

"Tobacco was ubiquitous throughout pre-Columbian America."

The First Smokers

Tobacco was ubiquitous throughout pre-Columbian America. The 12th-century Amerindian, though, didn't light up because the fish weren't biting or the stress of this week's deer quota was proving too much. Tobacco was regarded as one of the plants in which the spirit world was present; this was the reason for its hallucinogenic and healing powers. Ancient species of tobacco had nicotine contents many multiples greater than those found in present-day commercial types, and the shaman or medicine men inhaled lungful after lungful until they fell into a trance in which they were possessed by the spirits who gave them their curative powers. Tribes who preferred to chew tobacco often mixed it with lime or ash to facilitate nicotine release. Diagnosis of illnesses was achieved by blowing tobacco smoke over the patient's body. Tobacco leaves were stuffed into tooth cavities and ears to relieve pain; tobacco juice was squeezed on to wounds, then the wound was dressed with chewed leaves. The Mayas, Incas and Aztecs also used tobacco as a purging enema. About the only use tobacco never had was as a food – though its ability to supress appetite came in handy during times of food shortage. This therapeutic characteristic, if no other, continues to be cherished by the plumper, post-Columbian user.

"Holy plant or devilish herb? The debate is an old one."

Holy Smoke

Holy plant or devilish herb? The debate is an old one. An anonymous pamphleteer of 1602 argued (in *A Warning for Tobacconists*) that tobacco's origins in the heathen New World meant it was 'not to be used on us Christians'; the physician Leonardo Fioravanti countered that 'the plant ... has been revealed in this century for human health through the goodness of God.' A papal bull of 1642 banned the consumption of tobacco in church, and 17th-century theologians pondered whether the Blessed Sacrament was expelled after tobacco-induced sneezing or spitting, and whether tobacco constituted a food during Lent. It was, however, recommended for religious orders since, as Benedetto Stella observed in 1669, 'the natural cause of lust is heat and humidity. When this is dried out through the use of tobacco ... libidinous urges are not felt so powerfully.' Perhaps this happy insight lay behind the Church's conversion to tobacco's cause. Pope Benedict XIII ordained in 1725 that snuff might be taken in St Peter's to prevent 'the frequent walking out of those who can't abstain from the use of tobacco.' The final flourish came in 1779 when the Papacy opened its own tobacco factory. There is hope for condoms yet.

"Nicotiana is comparatively easy to grow in Britain."

Grow Your Own

Tobacco, along with potato, tomato, aubergine, foxglove and deadly nightshade, is one of the Scrophulariales. Nicotiana is not the only genus in the order to be used as a narcotic: American Indians employed Datura as a violent hallucinogen, while Australian Aborigines consumed pituri, leaves from the Duboisia genus, for mood-alteration. Nicotiana is comparatively easy to grow in Britain; many gardeners grow Nicotiana alata for its sweet-scented, dusk-opening flowers. Nicotiana tabacum, also known as Nicotiana gigantea, is the species used for tobacco production, and growing (and curing) your own is just as much your prerogative as making your own nettle-and-elderflower wine. Indeed, back in the 17th century, England had a domestic tobacco industry, originating in 1619, when two London merchants entered into a partnership to grow tobacco around the town of Winchcombe in Gloucestershire. Production initially centred on the Avon Valley and Vale of Evesham, but by 1655 tobacco was grown in 14 counties in England and Wales. Domestic production dwindled, however, faced with competition from the extensive Dutch fields (around 20 million pounds of tobacco per year were produced in Holland between 1700 and 1710) and from the Caribbean colonies. Now it's all up to you.

" ... one of the most splenetic texts ever penned by a monarch to his people."

A Royal Fume

It all got off to a very bad start. James I's *Counter-Blaste to Tobacco* must rank as one of the most splenetic texts ever penned by a monarch to his people. 'A custome lothsome to the eye, hateful to the Nose, harmefull to the braine, dangerous to the Lungs, and the blacke stinking fume thereof, neerest resembling the horrible Stygian pit that is bottomlesse,' concludes this scion of the House of Stuart's anti-smoking tract. The House of Hanover, in the person of Queen Victoria, also took against smoking to the extent of banning it at court. Edward VII, as one might expect from a man with 13 known mistresses, swiftly revoked the Victorian ban and is now associated with large cigars, thanks to the commercial tribute of a non-Havana brand. His grandson Edward VIII's humidor is in the possession of James J. Fox and Robert Lewis, the St James's cigar merchants. It was tobacco, however, which brought the reign of Edward VIII's brother George VI to an untimely end when he died from lung cancer aged 56. His elder daughter disdained the habit; his younger daughter did not. It is the Queen, not Princess Margaret, who has set the tone for the present royal family; none of the Princes, nor the Princess Royal, smokes. Mistresses are another matter.

"He raised the wrinkled object to his nose."

A Whiff of the Past

Whiff's monocle dropped reverentially. He raised the wrinkled object to his nose; we awaited his verdict. 'Nothing,' he said. 'Their odour has been dispersed by time, alas; the wonder of it is that they still exist at all.' He was handling one of the oldest cigars in the world: dark-wrapped torpedos made for the Great Exhibition of 1851, still lodged in the basement 'museum' of Fox/Lewis at 19 St James's St SW1 (0171 493 9009), which customers may visit by appointment. You can inspect Churchill's cigar accounts (paid) and Oscar Wilde's cigarette accounts (owing); you can see the original 1851 Lonsdales (commissioned by the Earl of Lonsdale); you can see early cartons of the Wingfield Tennis Smoking Mixture (a blend for Major Walter Wingfield, the lawn-tennis pioneer, and still sold upstairs in 50g tins); you can see the beautiful ceramic boxes in which Balkan Sobranies were packed by the thousand. Whiff pored over the final page of the Churchill accounts. 'All Romeo y Julieta,' he said, 'in three sizes: Alteza Grande, Epicure Grande and Piramides. Except for this: one purchase of Santa Marta Coronas Negras. Not one is available now — yet they abide,' he said, tapping a photograph of the great man.

"*That nocturnal cigarette would be his last. Paf!' Whiff's eyes widened.*"

Strike it Lucky

Cigarettes, unlike alcohol, are a palliative and source of solace which leaves both physical and mental abilities relatively unimpaired – hence their significance in wartime. A drunken soldier is no use; a smoking soldier remains fighting fit. 'Tommy loves Woodbines more than his grub,' the BAT Bulletin reported one Private Foden saying in 1916. Woodbines are remembered above all other brands as the Great War Smoke thanks chiefly to Geoffrey Studdert Kennedy MC, or Woodbine Willie as he was better known. Kennedy, a small, piano-playing, mildly dishevelled Irish Army chaplain distributed Woodbines to troops about to board the train to Rouen which would take them to the front. In many cases it was their last earthly comfort. Even Whiff is too young to have first-hand memory of this – though he does recall his own father telling him why it was unlucky to light three cigarettes from one match. 'Boer war, don't you know. The Boers were fine shots. If you struck a match in the darkness and kept it alight long enough to light three cigarettes, it gave the Boer marksman the moments he needed to get a fix on the third smoker. That nocturnal cigarette would be his last. Paf!' Whiff's eyes widened. He recalled, I saw, fire from the night.

"PH is the equatorial division of the smoking world."

Acid Test

Acid or alkaline? PH is the equatorial division of the smoking world, a consequence of both tobacco strain and curing method. Acidic smoke is what cigarettes produce, and its nicotine can only be absorbed by inhalation. Pipe and cigar tobacco, by contrast, is alkaline, and the nicotine in alkaline smoke can be absorbed through the mouth lining, thereby obviating the need to inhale. The lung-cancer risk diminishes, and the mouth-cancer risk rises. Absorption of nicotine through the mouth is a comparatively slow process, whereas nicotine races to the brain in just seven seconds when absorbed through the alveoli of the lung, and within 20 seconds has reached every part of the body. Speed of nicotine absorbtion is why those who switch away from cigarettes to pipes and cigars find it hard not to inhale. Tobacco smoke in general has a gaseous phase and a particulate (tar) phase, collectively containing over 4,700 compounds including hydrogen cyanide, cadmium, napthalene, arsenic and formaldehyde. Smoke inhaled directly through a cigarette contains fewer of these chemical compounds than smoke released into the air by the cigarette, confirming the fact that passive smokers get a very raw deal — more hydrogen cyanide, less nicotine.

"'Smoking kills', we read."

What's the Damage?

'Smoking kills,' we read. 'Tobacco seriously damages health.' 'Smoking causes fatal diseases.' The Chief Medical Officers have a busy time of it, getting into print on every piece of tobacco packaging and advertising. Why? Presumably the officers think that Britain is peopled by merry dimwits who believe that smoking prolongs life, or leads to greater fitness, or is just the ticket when pregnant in order to produce a bright-eyed nipper. In fact we all know that a packet of cigarettes a day will shorten our life, jeopardise our health and stunt our babies. Indeed this badness, many believe, lies somewhere near the core of the cigarette's appeal; the two fingers at death is indissolubly associated with the pleasures of the nicotine rush, with that taste of mellow autumn on the tongue. The warnings, by this logic, sharpen the smoker's commitment towards the evil weed, and lend smoking the sort of allure that other idiotically dangerous pastimes (motor racing, hang gliding, setting off up K2 at teatime) acquire. Their real function, of course, is to salve the government's own conscience as it rakes in tobacco-tax revenues.

" ... *sport loves tobacco because tobacco brings money.*"

Marques and Sponsors

Sport and tobacco do not naturally sing each other's song, or so you'd think. Tobacco loves sport because it gives it a chance to associate itself more clearly than advertising legislation permits with good times and health; and sport loves tobacco because tobacco brings money. The referee is the government, trying to stop these two entirely dissimilar beasts from embracing each other in intimate places to the embarrassment of all. The referee's rule book is a fudgy volume called The Voluntary Agreement, which is meant to help sport quit the tobacco habit but not so quickly that British sporting prowess and government tobacco tax revenues suffer. It is this agreement which dictates that British motor-racing circuits aren't allowed more than four signs per mile of track, nor cricket grounds more than three. Brands names are forbidden on cars, horses, dogs, players, officials and furniture. More meaningfully, tobacco sponsorship has been frozen at 1985 levels plus inflation. In 1993, for example, only £9 million from a total sports sponsorship budget of £250 million came from tobacco. Internationally, the picture is different, particularly for motor racing, a sport whose 'globality' and gluttonous appetite for money mean that its addiction is well beyond the reach of a governmental Nicorette or two.

"What of Whiff himself? 'In my armchair', he said, curtly."

Where To Do It?

Whiff had organised a colloquium: the six participants gathered in his rooms early one Saturday morning. 'Thank you, ladies and gentlemen, for your attendance at this early hour. Please light up. The topic under discussion is not universal smokeage — lost, I fear, forever; but what are the best, the very best, circumstances for a smoke?' The answers were many and varied. Whiff's nephew Roddy Whiff (Marlboro) argued for 'the fast lane of a quiet motorway at one in the morning.' 'Naked, in front of an open fire, after a bath,' was the pugnacious offering of Kim de Wynter, the much-pierced cigar connoisseur and middle-aged sapphist, formerly Whiff's accountant, for whom he maintained an unshakeable affection. I ventured, on behalf of pipe smokers, a forest stroll on a still, sunny day; Mrs Sludgett, a committed Embassy smoker when not 'doing' for Whiff and others, candidly admitted to the sofa and a good soap. Harry Whipper, Whiff's immensely wealthy hand-rolling landlord, liked to smoke while 'fixing things' at home in Croydon. What of Whiff himself? 'In my armchair,' he said, curtly. 'Notice, though, not one of these moments is under threat of prohibition. The private realm must remain sacrosanct.'

"'Have a game of chess, young fellow, won't you?'"

Abstaining

Something was wrong. Mrs Sludgett opened the door to Whiff's rooms when I knocked. 'I don't know what's the matter. It's terrible worrying, Mr J. I can't get a word out of him. Maybe you'll have more luck.' The great man was seated in front of a book I knew he treasured, *The Mineral Larder of the Abyssinian Highlands*, written by Major General Sir Studely Whiff. He was pale. Worse, the air was clear. 'Ah! It's you,' Whiff cried with a strangulated tone. 'Have a game of chess, young fellow, won't you?' It was more a statement than a question, and brooked no dissent. Only after Whiff lost two knights within 15 moves, a strategic collapse unparalleled in the history of our tussles, that I dared ask him if he was ... giving up. 'Giving up? Giving up? Ha!' He produced a sort of dry bark. 'Of course I'm not giving up, you fool. I'm simply enjoying, for a few days, the, um, pleasures,' (the word was cast in iron) 'of abstention.' Viewing the tight set of his lip, I thought it better to make no comment. My victory was absurdly easy. We sipped tea in silence.

" ... a doomed campaign to preserve the smoke-filled room."

Forest File

Forest is all about smokers' lib. Funded in large part by 'Britain's free-enterprise tobacco companies', this pressure group positions itself at the vanguard of libertarian thinking. In reality, though, it's little more than a noisy attempt to justify bad behaviour. Smoking is incontrovertibly anti-social. Good cigars and a few aromatic pipe tobaccos aside, tobacco smoke stinks (and never more so than when curling up from the modern, low-tar cigarette). Even smokers, many of whom prefer non-smoking flights, non-smoking trains and non-smoking offices, recognise this. What 'Britain's free-enterprise tobacco companies' should be spending their money on is communicating tobacco's extraordinarily rich culture and enumerating the ways in which, though inimical to physical health, it can bring solace to the obscure, complicated and terrifying business of being. Instead they are squandering it on a doomed campaign to preserve the smoke-filled room. The freedom to pollute and to infringe the liberty of others is not worth fighting for; the freedom to explore a culture, to refine pleasure and to express oneself in private as one wishes is altogether more important.

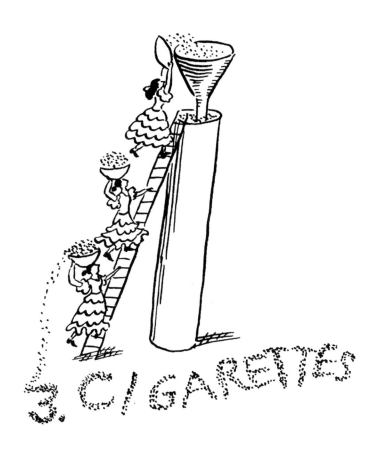

*"Early Gloag cigarettes ... were filled, using a funnel,
with powerful Turkish Latakia tobacco by Walworth girls."*

The Walworth Connection

The name Gloag is a familiar one to Scotch drinkers, being carried by the Grouse; it should be no less significant a name for cigarette smokers. Britain's first cigarette factory was established by one Robert Peacock Gloag in 1851 in Walworth. Gloag was an ex-paymaster to the Turkish forces in the Crimea, and it was during the Crimean War (1854-56) that Britons were first exposed to cigarettes by our Turkish and French allies. Early Gloag cigarettes had cane tips and yellow paper cases: they were filled, using a funnel, with powerful Turkish Latakia tobacco by Walworth girls. Early British brand names reflected these Crimean origins: Sultanas, Rifles, Zetlands, Operas and Moscows. Moscows, indeed, were a forerunner of the filter cigarette, having a piece of wool inserted at the end of the cigarette as an absorbant. Other companies capitalised on a growing market, including Wills in 1871 (whose first brand was Bristol). It was Wills who imported the first 'Bonsack' cigarette-making machines in 1883; these reduced the price of cigarettes greatly and led to a proliferation of brands. For a while, Passing Clouds proclaimed themselves 'Guaranteed hand-made,' but soon all was lost to the Bonsacks. The Carmens of Walworth were out on the street.

"Eventually, no doubt, cigarettes will contain nothing at all ... "

No Whiffs or Butts

Nothing has affected the manufacture and marketing of cigarettes more than the recognition that smoking causes lung cancer. Ninety-nine per cent of cigarettes smoked in Britain are now filter-tipped, for example, yet the first filter cigarette, Viceroy, was launched only in 1936 and enjoyed very modest sales for a decade or more. When the causal relationship between smoking and cancer was first suggested in 1954, Viceroy's sales promptly doubled; by 1960, half the cigarettes sold in America were filter-tipped. The manufacturers weren't unhappy, since they could sell customers less tobacco for the same price. A reduction in tar and nicotine levels is the other major consequence of tobacco's cancerous shadow. All cigarettes sold in the EC must now contain less than 15g of tar; in 1970, fewer than one per cent of cigarettes fell below this threshold. Again, manufacturers aren't complaining; the move to lighter flavour and a gentler kick means that they can use mildly flavoured reconstituted sheet (made from stems, scrap tobacco and tobacco dust) to a much greater extent than in the pre-Fifties 'Gold Flake' epoch. Eventually, no doubt, cigarettes will contain nothing at all, have no effect whatsoever and cost £10 a packet. Pass the cigars, please, someone.

"This leaves the short cigarette in dwindling supply."

Short Cuts

Two trends have dominated cigarette development over the last decade: tar and nicotine reduction, compensated by ever more grandiose lengths. King-size cigarettes have been overtaken by luxury length, themselves slightly shorter than superkings, which in turn have been exceeded by international cigarettes, finally capped by '120' versions (millimetres, of course). This leaves the short cigarette in dwindling supply. Player's No. 6 is no more; Gold Leaf is no more; Woodbine is rarer than the nightingale. Brands still guarding the flame of shortness (actually they're called 'regular' or 'standard') are led by Embassy and Embassy Regal; Silk Cut, too, has its origins in a regular (and thinner No. 3) which still sells well. France's Seita respects tradition in that its rich, warm tabac brun originals (Gitanes and Gauloises Disque Bleu) remain at standard length. Piccadilly No. 1 (plain) and Filter Deluxe are hanging on, but their tips must be on the block. Irish smokers, by contrast, still prefer their tobacco to remain within close lighting distance: Carroll's No. 1 is standard length, and so is Major. The latter, an informant tells me, has 'really taken off over the last two or three years.' The reason? 'Major is slightly thicker than most.'

"Since then, mentholated cigarettes ... have been the cool smoke for cool folk."

Cool Customers

In the beginning there was Kool. The year was 1933. Since then, mentholated cigarettes (outfitted, of course, in green) have been the cool smoke for cool folk. Sales of menthol cigarettes have doubled over the past five years, due to the hazy perception that they are low-tar; in fact they are mid-range, with 8-12mg. Pre-Kool, cigarettes could be mentholated by putting crystals of menthol, or blotting paper soaked in menthol, in cases and packets; nowadays either the tobacco or the wrapping papers are innoculated. Rothmans mentholates the wrapping paper for Consulate, St Moritz and Dunhill Menthol, for example, since this enables the company to use the same tobacco machinery for mentholated and non-mentholated brands alike. Reginald Whiff devoted an afternoon to the close scrutiny of six brands, and gave joint top marks to the gold-banded St Moritz and elegant newcomer YSL from Reynolds – both have sweet Virginia scents and creamy, smoothly mentholated flavours. Consulate pipped Salem for old-style fullness of flavour at a shorter length, while Dunhill and More smoked a mite too warm, according to the percipient Whiff, to evoke that celebrated mountain stream.

" ... all tobacco is 'toasted' in some way or other."

Lucky Draw

The history of great brand names is often curiously circuitous. Lucky Strike began as a brand of plug (chewing) and pipe tobacco, first registered in 1871 by a medical entrepreneur called Dr Patterson, who is said to have steeped the tobacco in his own patent cough syrup. By 1917, however, the cough mixture had been expunged and the brand assumed cigarette form. Then began a period of successful promotion built around the slogan 'It's toasted,' which still appears on the packet. (This is as daft as slogans generally are: all tobacco is 'toasted' in some way or other. 'It's rotting' is the only alternative.) Jean Harlow is said to have advertised Luckies for no fee; Douglas Fairbanks and Al Jolson also advertised the brand, and real-life heroes endorsed it, too. One Captain George Fried claimed Luckies helped him with 'nerve control' during a high-profile sea rescue. Bogart, as Sam Spade, stuck to Luckies throughout The Maltese Falcon, and the world's first 'hit parade' was featured on the Lucky Radio Show during the Thirties. Now you too can maintain your nerve control: the brand has been launched in Britain in Regular (13mg tar, 1mg nicotine) and Lights (9mg/0.8mg) formats. Toasted? Seems sweet and milky to me.

"Cowboys were roped in to help it towards a more macho image ... "

Strike a Pose

Marlboro was not always the cowboy's choice. What is today the world's biggest-selling cigarette made its early mileage by being sold as a luxury and then as a female cigarette. 'Women, when they smoke at all, quickly develop descriminating taste,' read the copy for a 1927 ad which showed an elegant miss demonstrating her powers of discernment by puffing on a Marly. Everything changed in the Fifties, after the cancer link was first established in 1954. Marlboro then became a filter cigarette and went into the red-and-white crushproof box familar today. Cowboys were roped in to help it towards a more macho image, combining fantasies of freedom, escape and heroic grandeur; this is the image which has powered it towards global domination. Formula One sponsorship helps the image, and seems likely to be even more crucial to manufacturers Philip Morris in the future as advertising restrictions cut back the potential for image creation. This has not been without its ironies, however: Alain Prost, a non-smoker who won three world championships under Marlboro colours, had to watch his brother (a heavy smoker) die of lung cancer. The original Marlboro cowboy, coincidentally called Wayne McLaren, also died of the same disease at 51. He was, by then, a passionate anti-smoking campaigner.

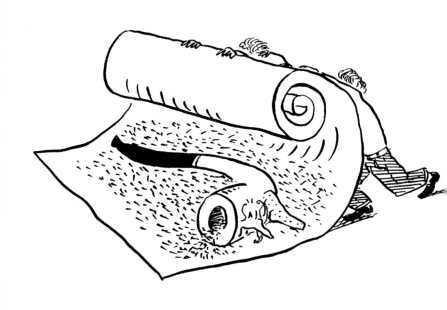

" … many loose, fine cuts of pipe tobacco are now feeling the roll."

Roll Up, Roll Up

You can make it your own way. It lasts longer. It tastes better. There aren't so many chemicals in it. It's cheaper. These are the justifications more than one in eight smokers will offer you, eyes lowered, as they roll tobacco wisps into fiddly papers to make shapeless, spindly, self-extinguishing cigarettes. Tobacconists report booming sales of r.y.o. tobacco. Scams abound, naturally. Estimates of the amount of hand-rolling tobacco currently being bootlegged in from across the Channel are as high as 15 per cent of total UK consumption. Then there is the legal scam: pipe tobacco duty is £36.30 per kilo, while cigarette tobacco duty is £85.90 per kilo. Consequently, many loose, fine cuts of pipe tobacco are now feeling the roll. Kendal Light, for example, ostensibly a 'mild pipe tobacco', is mysteriously purchased together with Rizla papers. Golden Virginia is still the king of official hand-rolling tobaccos, with over 50 per cent of the market, pursued at a respectful distance by Old Holborn. Gauloises is popular out on the intellectual fringe, and the Dutch Duma with Europhiles. Harry Whipper, Reginald Whiff's landlord, is an Old Holborn man. He finds it mellower than Golden Virginia, less ready to smart the eye, less adhesive on the curtains.

"To those who do, the purchase resonates with intimate preferences."

Paper Round

To those who don't roll, cigarette papers are mere stationery. To those who do, the purchase resonates with intimate preferences. Rizla Red is the Honest John of cigarette papers; there's also Rizla Blue (thinner), Green (with the nicked corner), sweet black Liquorice paper, and Ventaire (with tiny perforations for a cooler smoke). Red, Blue and Green come in king size, as does brown Wheetstraw, and we know which weed the king-sized papers get used for, don't we? (Clue: rhymes with Pope.) Connoisseurs hover between the exquisite Spanish 'Smoking' rice papers (which come in books of 33 extra-long, watermarked leaves) and Job, the traditional thicker paper, sold in double books; Rizla Originals now compete with this pair. Cañuma 'tree-free' hemp papers are the eco-choice; while the unbranded 'H.M.Prisons Only' (Rizla Red, in fact) brings street cred to those still defining themselves in terms of poll-tax evasion. The supremely dextrous, meanwhile, opt for Rips, a continuous roll of cigarette paper (Red is standard size, Green light-weight and Blue king size). Gauloises, Duma and Swan all produce their own papers, Swan's coming in the prettiest packets – and Swan, unlike Rizla, still offers the celebrated running-out slip, as the end approaches.

"American-style cigarettes ... account for over 70 per cent of the French market."

Blonde Ambition

C offee and croissants, Chanel No. 19, Parisian drains, garlicky breath: France has given the world as many great scents as any nation. Most of them exact maximum emotional pull, confirmed Francophiles aver, over a distant aromatic backdrop of dark cigarettes or *cigarettes brunes*. Who would prefer the trashy, ashy, throat-gagging reek of a Marlboro to the rich, savoury, farmyard aroma of a Gauloise Brune? Alas, the average Frenchman now would, it seems. Light-tobacco American-style cigarettes – *les blondes* – account for over 70 per cent of the French market, while warm Gallic *brunes* are down to 29 per cent. The biggest-selling single brand, to be sure, is still Gauloises Brunes with 20 per cent, but Marlboro (17 per cent) and Gauloise's own *blondes* (8 per cent) are on its tail. Indeed Gauloises Blondes look set to overtake Gitanes Brunes at any moment. Light cigarettes (less than 10mg of tar) are also on the rise: 35 per cent of the French market and growing, with Gauloise itself available as a *léger* and an *ultra-léger*. Meanwhile that great stinking, smudgy, stop-go bonfire of a cigarette, the Boyard, is a sad victim of European legislatory madness: it has proved impossible to accommodate it within the EC 15mg tar ceiling. *Mes amis*, the Boyard is no more: weep for France.

"'So why were you in France anyway?' I asked."

Secret Agent

'Seen this?' said Whiff, tossing a packet of unfiltered Gauloises on to the table. They'd been bought in France, but I couldn't spot anything startling about them. 'You mean the health warning?' I queried. 'Smoking discredits your entourage?' 'No, no, not that at all. Look at the side, next to the nicotine and tar. Typical of Johnny Frenchman, what? He actually tells you how much tobacco you're getting: 90.5 per cent in this case. Cigarette paper is 4.5 per cent and *agents de texture* come in at 5 per cent. Why don't our lot do that, eh? Afraid of telling us, I expect. Like those great British bangers which turn out to be filled with bread. *Agents de texture*, indeed!' Whiff sat down in his armchair, opened the softpack and tapped out a Gauloise. Its warm, farmyardy scent filled the air. 'So why were you in France anyway?' I asked. 'Sort of reunion, old boy. The war, don't you know? I promised Buffy I'd go down to see our chaps.' He smoked on, thoughtfully. I made one last try. 'What chaps, Whiffy?' He laughed softly, but then grew serious. 'Our *agents. Mais pas de texture. Ça, non. Pas du tout.*' I couldn't get any more out of him. But his French accent was startlingly good.

" ... *during a night in the restless and downy arms of a Balkan princess* ... "

Young Turks

Gone, all gone. Or almost. The great Turkish and Oriental cigarette tobaccos of the past have been sacrificed in the spurious quest to make a fundamentally unhealthy habit marginally less unhealthy. As tar and nicotine levels have been lowered, aroma and flavour have been stripped out of cigarettes, too. Tobacco entrepreneur Mark Acton of Tor Imports is determined to reverse the decline: following a series of trial blends, backed by smoke samplings held in conjunction with St James's tobacconists Fox/Lewis, he has commissioned two new filter brands from a Belgian manufacturer. Tor Turkish uses Izmir and Samsun together with other Turkish tobaccos, and Tor Oriental blends Middle Eastern strains with leavening Virginia and Burley; both meet EC tar and nicotine limits. Reginald Whiff, who once claimed to have smoked Turkish cigarettes on the Orient Express during a night in the restless and downy arms of a Balkan princess, put them to the test. 'Tor Oriental smells – unlit – extraordinarily rich, almost raisiny; it smokes suprisingly mildly, sweetly, an elegant Mozartian rendition of its musky Asiatic prototype. Tor Turkish is sweet and heady, too, but with greater spiciness of aroma and a fuller, more savoury flavour.' Both brands are now permanent accoutrements in Whiff's Pall Mall rooms.

"'Whiff here. Got something to show you. Pop over when you can.'"

Matchless Ovals

The phone rang. 'Whiff here. Got something to show you. Pop over when you can.' The line went dead. I had, however, detected excitement in the curt tone the great smoker adopted for telephonic communications. I reached Pall Mall at dusk. Mounting the stairs, I could hear a scratched '78 recording of Nermin Inalcik, the great Turkish crooner of the Thirties, filling the Whiff apartment with sinuously brilliantined melodies. He paced briskly to the door and shook his cigarette in my face. 'They're back,' he cried in triumph. 'Plain ovals. Oriental blend. Smell them, by jove, smell them.' He produced a box of George Karelias and Sons Oriental Plain Ovals and thrust them under my nose. 'Raisins, what? Creamy; perfumed. And bits in the mouth.' I took one, rocked its oval unevenness between my fingers, and sniffed: it was indeed sweet and rich, like the smell of crushed figs on a sunny, stony path. Whiff retreated; Nermin let out a honeyed wail.

"'Sometimes', said Freud himself, 'a cigar is just a cigar.'"

Freudian Slip

Any catalogue of this century's most famous smokers would be certain to include the names Winston Churchill, Humphrey Bogart, Reginald Whiff — and Sigmund Freud. 'Contact [during psychoanalysis],' wrote Freud's colleague Raymond de Saussure, 'was established only by means of his voice and the odour of the cigars he ceaselessly smoked.' Freud viewed them 'as protection and a weapon in the combat of life ... I owe to the cigar a great intensification of my capacity to work and a facilitation of my self-control.' One word for food in German is *lebensmittel*, 'lifestuff'; Freud called cigars *arbeitsmittel*, 'workstuff'. He smoked from the age of 24 until his death at 83, despite contracting cancer of the soft palate (a condition undoubtedly related to his smoking) when he was 67. What, though, is one to make of the man who rejuvenated, in modern times, the notion of the phallic symbol, and introduced that of penis envy, spending most of his waking life sucking on an object whose exact dimensions, fine surface veins and rich animal smell makes it the most obvious of all substitutes for the male organ of generation in procreational mode? 'Sometimes,' said Freud himself, 'a cigar is just a cigar.'

"Unseemly squabbles ... in the corridors of wealth and privilege."

Cuban Crisis

Unseemly squabbles are breaking out in the corridors of wealth and privilege. Cigar men are locked in wallet-to-wallet combat. The dread spectre of famine haunts the humidors. Cuba's tobacco farmers had a miserable start to the Nineties, with '91, '92 and '93 each yielding around 50 million cigars rather than the 80 million the market wants. This was due to poor weather combined with shortages of fertilizer, cheesecloth (essential for growing wrapper leaf) and string. Nineteen-ninety-four was a splendid vintage, but the shortages persisted, so Cubatobaco asked its distributors to help with hard-currency loans. This they did, achieving a 20 per cent improvement in yield for the '95 harvest (despite a devastating storm on 12 January, which flooded the Hoyo de Monterrey plantation). Because all hand-made Cuban cigars contain leaf from at least three separate harvests, the improvements from '94 and '95 won't filter through until '97. Large, long cigars have been hardest hit. No matter: particularly savourous at present, Whiff reports, are the mid-sized Punch Punch, the El Rey del Mundo Choix Supreme and the fashionable Hoyo de Monterrey Epicure No. 2.

"Then come total fakes: imitations of Davidoff and Cohiba ... "

Faking It

The cigar world is confusing. Purchasers of hand-made Havana Upmanns or Partagas in Britain may be caught out elsewhere in Europe where machine-made versions of apparently identical cigars are sold. Then come total fakes: imitations of Davidoff and Cohiba, still said to be on sale in the duty-free shop at São Paolo, not to mention fakes from Cuba itself. Visitors to Havana are likely to be offered apparently authentic boxes of Cohiba cigars, constructed from scraps of leaf and box smuggled out of the factories, at 'give-away' prices. Deception is also practised on a wider scale; one wealthy London collector dispatched his chauffeur to the Canary Islands to purchase a bargain parcel of Cohiba Lanceros, which proved on smoking to be fakes; and a London auction house recently rejected a large parcel of Davidoff Dom Pérignon and Cohiba Lanceros, fearing inauthenticity. No fewer than six 'hallmarks' are to be found on genuine hand-made Havanas sold in Britain: the Cubatobaco emblem, and the phrases *Hecho en Cuba* (made in Cuba) and *Totalmente a mano* (completely by hand) branded into the base of the box; the Cuban government warranty seal; the 'EMS' label, indicating that the box has been imported directly to Britain; and the red Habanos chevron.

"These are splendid nursery cigars."

The Nursery Cigar

If Cuba is to cigars what France is to wine, then the Dominican Republic offers the New World-like virtues of unrivalled softness and creaminess – at a price discount. Dunhill has switched all its hand-made cigar production to the Dominican Republic, Cuba having ceased to manufacture brands of non-Cuban ownership. The vintage-dated Dunhill Aged Cigar range is composed of Dominican filler and binder leaf in Connecticut shade wrapper. These are splendid nursery cigars. The tubed Altamiras (a Robusto size) is gentle to the end, its aromas suggesting milky coffee and toast, its flavour sapidly silky. It is with the tubed Cabreras (a Churchill size) that the Dominican cigar is at its most orchestral: a lusher mixture of raisins and chocolate relieved by a fresh-cut grassiness. The draw is good – Consolidated Cigar, the manufacturers, have a top-secret sucking machine to draw-test each cigar – and quality is more consistent than with Cuban exports. If badly stored, however, Dominican cigars can be dull and dry-grassy in flavour, and they are rarely profound or dark. At time of writing, Dunhill is moving between the 1989 and 1994 vintages, the intermediate years having been found wanting. As with wine, one bad summer can spoil your swallow.

"'Where's the sense of wild adventure, dammit?'"

Brit Blend

The quest for a sapid cigar from the Dominican Republic continues. Latest entrant to the lists is a range of four sizes from Santa Damiana (panatelas, petit coronas, coronas and churchills). These, the importers claim, have been specifically rolled for the British market following smoking tests on nine trial leaf blends; the final version uses richly flavoured leaf from the middle and tops of plants grown in the Cibāo valley as filler, finished with brown Connecticut wrapper. Whiff spotted the latter immediately. 'American,' he said. 'Darker than it can be, but look at that fine-veined, mono-hued uniformity. Well-rolled, steady draw, technically correct — we expect that from the Dominican Republic, though. Begins a little hesitantly, but finds its feet well: there is coffeeish flavour here, and a push for depth.' He smoked on. 'A mite monotonous by half-time. Where's the sense of wild adventure, dammit? Where's the unpredictability? Still, it's nice to be able at least to taste a Dominican for a change.' He laid the butt to rest.

"'A little Cuban birdie told me. Exciting, isn't it?'"

Torpedoed

'Have you heard?' I asked Whiff breathlessly, having run all the way up the stairs. 'About the new Havanas?' 'You mean Cuaba, I suppose,' he replied languidly. He could see I was crestfallen; I had hoped to break the news to him. 'I've only just heard,' he said, with a conciliatory tone. 'A little Cuban birdie told me. Exciting, isn't it? They're all going to be torpedo shaped – or *figurado* as the Cubans say. You'll recall that those nineteenth-century cigars in the Fox/Lewis museum are pointed at both ends; the fashion for torpedoes died out in the 1930s. I understand the new brand will consist of four sizes, varying from four to five inches long – of course, both ends will need cutting. *Cuaba*, apparently, is an old Taino Indian word signifying a sort of burning bush they have on the island. It's an interesting development: we may well see more new brands from Cuba, as a way of avoiding the existing problems over disputed trademark names. My little birdie told me the launch is to be in London, in November. It promises to be an incandescent affair. Hope we get asked,' he added, wistfully. 'I'm sure your birdie can fix it,' I replied, curtly.

" ... *to the envious amazement of three tipsy travellers and a pelican* ... "

Coffee-Break Cigars

How long is yours? The advent of the smoke-free workplace means that those who wish to maintain a relationship with Nicotiana tabacum are out on the street for the duration. Cigarettes zip along breezily enough; cigars linger longer. Reginald Whiff agreed to step out from his befugged Pall Mall rooms into St James's Park where, to the envious amazement of three tipsy travellers and a pelican, he smoke-tested seven small brands simultaneously. Swiftest, at nine minutes, was Winterman's Café Crème, loose-packed and harsh. Aromatically richer, though over-tight on the draw, was the Romeo y Julieta Small: 15 minutes of hot Havana. the Panter Vitesse went to 18 minutes, but its flavours of Continental roast coffee were more after-dinner than mid-morning. It exceeded Rio 6 by a minute, though Rio 6's rich, animal style and soft draw were more soothing. Panter Mignon is a 23-minute upgrade of the nimble Vitesse. Do you have 31 minutes for a Villiger Export? It's a mild, calmingly aromatic smoke with a spicy finish. The hand-made Petit Upmann is a rich, dark, complex cigar, but who – Whiff, the travellers and a pelican apart – has 48 minutes for a coffee break?

"Slow-burning, excruciatingly flavoursome ... "

Cheroots

Together with bidis (see page 101), India's wispy, thread-tied roll-ups, the cheroot is one of Asia's distinctive contributions to tobacco culture. Although the word is of Tamil origin, Burma cheroots (like Pue No.2 and No.8, and Scotts No.5) led the market in the Forties and Fifties. The last true Burma cheroot still marketed here is the beautifully packaged Jade, available in packets of five or ten. Tissue-wrapped, dark-leaved, resolutely slow-burning, Jade's Burma tobacco combines coconut sweetness with a heavy-lidded, cow-byre muskiness. The word cheroot subsequently came to describe any cigar cut untapered at both ends (so, for example, the square-pressed Swiss-German Rio 6 might qualify). Truer if more wicked heirs of the Burma cheroot, though, are Italian cheroots like Toscanelli or the handsomely packaged Toscanero: densely packed, black-tobacco cigars in small, knobbly, pyramid shapes (leaf veins included). Slow-burning, excruciatingly flavoursome (lag your tongue with milk first to withstand their bitter-coffee onslaught), they constitute a heroically uncompromising variant on slow Burmese indulgence.

" ... *which reminded many of his woodsman customers of the logs they felled ...* "

Square Deals

Whiff and I find ourselves mired in controversy following the appearance of Rio 6 and Villiger Export in a short text concerning the cheroot (see page 73). 'These cigar brands', writes a learned reader, 'owe their origin to a very different, European heritage of cigar making. They are *stumpen*.' Flashback to 1870 or so, when an inventive Swiss cigar-maker called Ormond hit on the idea of producing cigars not by rolling them individually, but by making a triple-length cigar and cutting it into sections. Such cigars, of course, have straight, not rounded, ends, which reminded many of his woodsman customers of the logs (*stumpen*) they felled in order to pay for their tobacco habit. Jean Villiger, in 1888, noted Ormond's success and opened a factory for *stumpen* production; Ormond's, by the way, closed in 1993. The distinctive square shape of Rio 6 and Villiger Export was the consequence of a fashion for pressed Havanas in the Thirties, which *stumpen* manufacturers naturally followed. Villiger Export comes in square (*gepresst*) and round (*rund*) form. Reginald Whiff has long maintained that the square version, although blended from the same tobacco, tastes slightly milder than the round one. 'Whiff may be right,' admits Simon Chase of Hunters & Frankau, Villiger's British agent. 'The square *stumpen* fit tightly together during the drying process, and the raised temperature provokes a slight further fermentation. This could produce an effect of mildness.'

"' … he was taken poorly during the Queen's Speech.'"

Christmas Puff

'What,' I asked Whiff, noting him busily arranging his seven Christmas cards on the mantelpiece, 'should I furnish Uncle Eustace with this Christmas? He only smokes one cigar a year, after Christmas lunch, and my job is to supply it. Last year I gave him a Bolivar Belicosos Finos and he was taken poorly during the Queen's Speech.' Whiff guffawed. 'Not surprised, dear boy: if a chap has just one smoke a year, you've got to go easy on the flavour. Size-wise, I'd opt for a Petit Corona or a Corona; there's only half an inch between them, and they'll both give blessed Eustace the best part of an hour's smoking pleasure. The Upmann Petit Corona is mild as milk yet intricate, too. If he's looking frisky, try him on a Romeo y Julieta tubed No.2 or a Montecristo Petit Tubos. For a longer haul I'd go for the Punch Royal Coronation or, even better, the lovely Romeo y Julieta tubed No.1. There's such grace in that cigar.' His illustrative gesture sent the Christmas cards flying.

"Bands ... became a cheap way of lending a cut-price cigar allure."

The Band

Strangely enough, I'd never thought about it before. It was when Whiff got out his 'oddments box' — a collection of bundle ends and solitaires — and offered me the pick of them that I found myself wondering about the origin of the cigar band. 'I've heard various hare-brained stories concerning Catherine the Great and silk-wrapped cigars,' said Whiff, 'but the truth seems to be that the practice was initiated in Cuba in the 1830s by a German, Gustave Bock, who was concerned about the widespread counterfeiting of his brand in Europe. Within 20 years, all Cuban cigars carried bands and European and American cigar producers followed suit. They became a cheap way of lending a cut-price cigar allure. They even became a sort of Green Shield Stamp. In the early years of this century, the American Cigar Co. offered a redemption scheme: 600 bands gave you a year's subscription to *Scientific American*, and 180,000 a baby grand piano.' Whiff had, by now, removed his band and tossed it on the fire. 'You never smoke with the band in place?' I enquired, timidly. 'Good heavens, no,' replied Whiff, 'and I never purchase monogrammed clothes, either. The quality should be evident,' he sighed, leaning back, 'in the smoke.'

"'My preference', lectures Whiff, 'is for the guillotine.'"

A Mere Snip

Good, hand-made cigars are closed at one end, using either a piece of leaf called a cap, or with a specially shaped part of the wrapper leaf called a flag (flags are often formed into twists at the end of a cigar). Smoking such cigars, of course, requires cutting the ends first. The main ways of cutting cigars are with one's teeth, with guillotine cutters, with cigar scissors, with V-cutters, or with piercing devices which cut or bore a hole in the cap or flag. 'My preference,' lectures Whiff, 'is for the guillotine. Teeth rarely incise with the requisite surgical exactitude: the great aim is to avoid tearing or unravelling the wrapper and binder. If you want a cheap cut, try a scalpel. Scissors may waggle and botch unless supremely sharp: the energy is applied too far from the cigar's end. V-cutters or wedge-cutters are over-complicated, and a bad V-cut can smoke hot. Piercers and bull's-eyes may grind the filler about and provide too small a hole. Among guillotines, I prefer the single blade to the double, but sharpness is all. You cut just below the cigar's shoulder, so that a small portion of the cap or flag still partly enfolds the filler leaves. Store cutters carefully, of course, to avoid infants performing digital decapitation on each other.'

"'Dribbling should be avoided at all costs.'"

How to Smoke a Pipe

'In my day,' grumbled Reginald Whiff, 'young ladies rarely smoked pipes. Still, no reason why they shouldn't. What the hell! I'll give it a go.' Thus it was, that, a year or two ago, Whiff was cajoled into giving a pipe-smoking masterclass to the Vauxhall Gay Women's Cooperative at the invitation of its events animator (and Whiff's former accountant), the much-pierced Kym de Wynter. 'Fill it full but don't overpack it,' counselled the sage. 'There should always be spring in the leaf. If you can't use a taper, remember that the first match will singe the tobacco, but does not light the pipe; that is the duty of the second match. Pull steadily until you have obtained sound combustion.' He leaned back into the soft leather bean bag, wreathed in grey. 'The skilled smoker masters the art of gentle outpuffing through the pipe following the drawing in of smoke; this enables the nostrils to tug in the often sweet external fumes of a good tobacco. The creation of downdraught with the two forefingers or a matchbox is permissable in case of failing combustion, though inelegant. Avoid relighting; it predisposes to acridity. Tap out the bolus of ash against wood or glass. Dribbling should be avoided at all costs. Any questions?' A clamour ensued; and the event is now an annual fixture in the cooperative calendar.

"Apple ... is the classic, basic pipe ... "

Dream Pipes

You could just march in and say 'I'd like a pipe, please.' If you really want to win admiration, however, try this: 'Could I look at a bent Apple or a bent Rhodesian with a root or dress finish?' The assistant will purr like a well-stroked cat as you trot out pipeman's arcana of this sort. Good pipes all begin with a lump of briar root (briar being a wild, shrubby relative of heather). The older, the better: Dunhill claims its pipes are often made from centenarian briar. The strange terminology cited above has developed to describe the final shape. Apple, for example, is the classic, basic pipe; Chimney, Canadian, Liverpool and Billiard are more voluminous; Rhodesian and Bulldog have waisted bowls; Pot is squatter and fatter; Prince and Diplomat taper towards the top. A bent pipe falls away from the lips in best Holmesian style; most of the above pipes are also available in bent versions. Among truly ludicrous pipes one must count the Hungarian, a huge-bowled bent of absurdly jutting style; and the Calabash, which looks like a lurid yellow ear trumpet. Finishes to the briar vary from the sombre, dark 'dress' to the pale, glowing 'root', where the wood's mottled grain is visible.

" ... a smoker might get through half a dozen or so per day."

Pipes of Clay

Between 1600 and 1850, the English enjoyed tobacco almost exclusively through the narrow conduit of a clay pipe. Or pipes: their fragility meant that a smoker might get through half a dozen or so per day. The size of the bowl bore a direct relationship to the cost of tobacco, which is why Elizabethan clays have tiny bowls. A clay pipe can provide a mightily hot mouthful; the clay warms as the tobacco burns, and rounded stem ends deliver the smoke on to a single spot on the tongue which increases the mordant effect. Clays, by the way, can be cleaned via an informal re-baking in an open fire. It was durability which saw the clay pipe eclipsed by the briar and meerschaum. The last English producer of clay pipes, Pollock of Manchester, was taken over by snuff makers Wilson's of Sharrow in the Eighties; Wilson's continues to produce clays using the Pollock moulds. For maximum historical *frisson*, arm yourself with an 18-inch churchwarden. The elegance of this pale clay is unmatched; its fragility adds a patina of danger to the combustive performance, and every added inch cools the smoke further. Size has its uses.

*"but not before the ... carvers have
worked on the still-malleable, moistened mineral."*

White Smoke

'**H**ydrated magnesium silicate,' beamed Whiff through a cloud of Dunhill's 965. 'Also knows as sepiolite. The German name means 'sea foam', since it appeared foamy when found on the Black Sea. This, though,' he said, waving the sculpted meerschaum pipe about which I had enquired so innocently, 'was mined around Eskisehir in Turkey, the world's major commercial deposit. It's soft when they bring it up: indeed in pre-pipe days it was used to make a primitive washing lather. The air hardens it, but not before the Turkish carvers have worked on the still-malleable, moistened mineral. It is finished by immersion in boiling beeswax, and the finest may be fitted with an amber stem. Smoking usage, thanks to the beeswax finish, gradually turns it from snow white to a soft plum brown, thereby increasing the pipe's value greatly.' I pointed out that Whiff's was streaky. 'Doesn't happen evenly,' he said, a mite testily. 'It's a long business; I've been at this one, on and off, for the best part of twenty years. It may be,' he continued in a lowered voice, 'that *others* may be called upon to finish my work after I am gone.' 'Oh,' I said, nonplussed.

"'If it's good enough for Popeye ... then it's good enough for me.'"

Corn Clot

Whiff smiled, and I knew I had lost my bet. It was undertaken lightly enough — a £10 wager that he had never smoked a corncob pipe. 'If it's good enough for Popeye,' he replied with a gleam in his eye, 'then it's good enough for me.' He returned with not one but a dozen or so: 'You need to buy them in bulk, since they don't last. They were an American Indian tradition, first produced commercially in the mid-nineteenth century by the firm which still makes them today, puzzlingly called the Missouri Meerschaum Company. Since 1946, they have been produced from a very woody, hybrid corn, aged for two years before shaping. All are finished with a plaster-of-Paris paste, and the best are varnished and shellacked. Trouble is, they all burn out.' He showed me the evidence. I pointed, with amusement, to an outsized version. 'That's a big Mac,' he said. 'Tell me why, and I'll annul your gambling debt.' A wartime photo came to mind. 'General MacArthur, perhaps?' 'Dammit', he said, smiling and twirling the tips of his moustache. 'You're not as stupid as you look.'

"Hand-blending is still practised by a few tobacconists ... "

Mixed Bags

When did you last have a shag? Or a plug, come to that? How about a Latakia-rich mixture, a flake based on red Virginia, or a ready-rubbed flavoured with Louisiana perique? The pipe-tobacco blender's culture is as rich as the whisky blender's. Its basic divisions are a consequence of curing method: flue or machine curing (as for Virginia tobaccos); fire curing, often over woodsmoke (as for oak- or pine-infused Latakia from Syria, or hickory-infused Kentucky); air curing, the gentlest of the methods (used for Burley tobaccos and dark, air-cured French types); and sun curing (used for Oriental tobaccos). Some pipe tobaccos are also heated and pressed – like spicy perique, which macerates in its own juices, or sugar-flavoured Cavendish types. The cut may be a flake (sliced from a pressed block – or you could flake your own from a plug) or ready-rubbed cut from a flake. Extra-fine cuts (suitable for clay pipes and roll-ups) are shags. Hand-blending is still practised by a few tobacconists, such as Dunhill, 30 Duke St, London SW1. Flavoured aromatics have proved popular of late, though classic pipe-men frown on such gimmickry, preferring to trace the autumnal darknesses and vegetal cadenzas of, say, Dunhill's 'Mr Alfred's Own'.

" *... dancing with an almond-eyed waitress from Streatham ...* "

'Erbal Warning

Summer was almost over, and Whiff looked dark. 'What's up, old stick?' I asked. 'Twenty years ago, I'd have been in Monte Carlo with Clarissa Overend or Buffy Wigg-Pitt,' the venerable socialite replied. 'No one spent August in London, dammit.' He subsided into sentimental gloom. Noting with alarm the fact that his lighter was untouched on the table and the air was ominously fresh, I tentatively suggested the Notting Hill Carnival. He brightened a little. 'But what should I smoke?' he asked, plaintively. I explained what others were likely to be smoking, which provoked a new crisis of confidence in the conservative septuagenarian. We finally decided that Whiff was to take his finest calabash – a bright yellow trumpet pipe – and smoke a scented combination of the gentle, vanilla-haunted Alsbo Black and the exotic Borkum Riff Cherry Cavendish. It was a success. 'Natty pipe, grandad,' boomed one bead-festooned reveller. 'What's your weed, man?' asked another. Pouches were compared and leaf exchanged; the new blend gave Whiff such peculiar satisfaction that he ended up dancing with an almond-eyed waitress from Streatham, his calabash clenched between his teeth and a tin of Red Stripe in each hand. The date is now a permanent fixture in the Whiff diary.

"'Where are the bonfires of yesteryear, eh? Answer me that.'"

Remember, Remember...

'Time was,' drawled Reginald Whiff, hands thrust deep into his pockets, looking out on to the last autumn leaves blowing about St James's Park, 'when I'd go down to the Wigg-Pitt's pile every year for Guy Fawkes' night. Buffy used to dress the Guy up as Hitler, and we'd take pot shots at the blighter before the fire was lit. Lavinia used to be a bit iffy about smoke, you know, in her 'withdrawing room', so we used to smoke like funnels out by the fire. I can see Buffy now, striding about in the gloom and the drizzle like a tugboat, his pipe stuffed full of the blackest flakes. I used to prefer a double corona — easier to get the damn thing lit.' Whiff got out his cigarette case slowly, tapping and then lighting a plain Player's. 'Saw Buffy a month or two back, in that nursing home place. Bloody shame, it was. Brought him down an ounce or two of Baby's Bottom, light as milk, and we'd just lit up when some harridan charged in saying Buffy couldn't smoke because he always set his pyjamas ablaze. We had a go at getting out through the window but Buffy got stuck on the sill, dammit.' Whiff exhaled, into low sunlight. 'Where are the bonfires of yesteryear, eh? Answer me that.'

"British hopes have not been extinguished."

Pipe Teams

So we came fiftieth. It could have been worse: there were 92 teams in all. There is, though, as our boys admit, certainly room for improvement. Best English time in the International Pipe Smoking competition was 54 minutes for the three grams achieved by London-based Peter Wiseman. Heroic; but nonetheless a long way adrift of the winning time from the Italian champion, the redoubtable Claudio Cavicchi, who puffed in at a sensational two hours 43 minutes and 53 seconds thanks to some nimble work with the tamper. Female pipe-smokers should take heart from the fact that second place went to Belgium's head-turning Marina de Wolf, who managed to keep her fire burning for two hours 35 minutes. Our squad (the other two team members were Norwich's Len Ellis and Plymouth's Andrew Briggs) are honing their techniques for next year. In particular, the Italian stratagem of shredding the tobacco as finely as possible during the five-minute filling time, then packing it tightly into the pipe, appears to be the key the attaining the elusive goal of a three-hour, three-gram smoke. British hopes have not been extinguished. We mean to light them on the beaches ...

"Never be seen without them at ... motorway protest demos."

Old Bidis

The bidi ('something rolled' in Hindi) is a genuinely primeval smoke. A wispy rolled tendu leaf enclosing a chopped salma-gundi of other plant leaves, it's the kind of thing which would look more than credible on the lips of a 14th-century Caribbean hunter-gatherer. Today, it is low-caste and rural Indians who smoke bidis; the metropolitan elite prefer cigarettes of varying degrees of dubiety and toxicity. In Europe, bidis containing tobacco leaf stumble over so many EU tobacco regulations that they are only available on an under-the-counter basis (Southall, where they arrive by the suitcase-load, is the best place to find them). Mint bidis, how-ever, are officially marketed, being classified as herbal cigarettes. In fact the difference between the mint bidi and the ordinary bidi is not great, since tobacco is only a minor component of bidis. Mint bidis contain spearmint, marjoram, gigantic swallowwort, holy basil, papaya and sour orange leaf, all wrapped in tendu leaf and tied, by the impoverished ladies who make them, with thread. The draw is variable, but a well-wrapped mint bidi smokes richly and sweetly, only resembling a bonfire in its final third. Never be seen without them at solstice festivals or motorway protest demos.

"Whiff is sceptical, though I tell him it's all innocent fun."

Mixing It

My paternal grandfather, a man who died of little more than exhaustion in his nineties, was a lifelong pipesmoker who, when it became apparent that tobacco was not entirely the familiar friend it had always been assumed to be, switched to herbal mixtures. He seemed to enjoy them just as much as tobacco, the main thrust of his pleasure being the ability to produce a large enough cloud of smoke to obscure his chair from the rest of the room. He smoked ready-made herbal mixtures, but there is nothing to stop you compounding your own. My experiments suggest that a mixture of herbs and tobacco is ideal: dry the fresh herb, leaf or petal in the sun, then moisten and aromatise it if you wish with honey, wine, cognac or whisky. Among the garden herbs you can use in this way are lavender, hyssop, chamomile, lemon balm, mint and thyme; raspberry leaves, birch leaves and lobelia leaves (sometimes known as Indian tobacco) can also be called into combustible service, as can rose petals and hops. Liquorice and angelica root can be grated into your mixture, and aniseed sprinkled. Whiff is sceptical, though I tell him it's all innocent fun. Get planting.

"What do barristers, clergymen and miners have in common?"

Feeling the Pinch

What do barristers, clergymen and miners have in common? They all work in environments which preclude the roll-up glued to the lower lip. So inveterate tobacco users among them sniff snuff. Snuff is tobacco leaf ground up, matured for between two and eight weeks, and often flavoured with aromatic oils. For example, Smith's Golden Cardinal (from the Snuff Shop, 74 Charing Cross Road, London WC2) has a clear whiff of the thurible to it. George IV is a spicy snuff. Café Royale is coffee-based. For an unflavoured snuff, choose SP Best. Wilson's of Sharrow (P.O. Box 32, Sheffield) produces Cinnamon, Burgundy, Carnation and souk-soaked Grand Cairo among others. A snuff-taking friend of Reginald Whiff's owns to taking the mentholated Hedges L260 for its breezily evacuative effect on the cranial chambers. Frebourg & Treyer's brands tend to geographical inspiration: they include Bordeaux, Old Paris and Seville. One question haunts the grinders: will the advent of the global smoke-free zone see a renaissance in snuff-taking? They're keeping their fingers pinched.

"Masticators will find a warm welcome in Stockholm."

Biting Back

Of all the ways of getting nicotine into the bloodstream, few have suffered as total an eclipse as chewing tobacco. The British tradition, once vigorous among the mining community, was for plug-like tobaccos such as Irish Pigtail Twist — a strong, oily and bitter chew for those with hair on their tongues. In America, the hillbilly legacy has remained lively longer, and sweetened, flavoured brands like Red Man, Beech Nut and Apple Jack make an easier entry into the palate-wrecking pleasures of the chew. Most curious of all is the gobbet known as 'dipping snuff'. This is a coarse, black, gelatinous cut that is rolled in a ball in the fingers and then inserted between lip and gum, where it lingeringly dissolves, aided by copious spitting. Dipping snuff is now banned in the EU, owing to its villainous propensity to cause mouth cancer — except, that is, in the case of new-boy Sweden, which to stave off popular unrest obtained 'a permanent exception' to the rule prior to entry this January. Known as *snus* in Swedish, dipping snuff has long been popular among working Swedes — more popular, indeed, than cigarettes until after the Second World War. The Scandinavian propensity for this vice is reflected in the fact that American brands of dipping snuff pass under names like Copenhagen and Skol. Masticators will find a warm welcome in Stockholm.

"Reginald Whiff professes horror at the prospect."

Coming from Behind

The clay pipe and snuff box are more often seen in museums than homes nowadays; a still rarer vehicle of tobacco administration is the clyster. This was a device designed to facilitate the rectal ingestion of tobacco, either as smoke or as a liquid infusion – a widespread practice from the arrival of the weed on European shores until the mid-19th century. Tobacco was taken anally by American Indians to cure diarrhoea, and the clyster, too, was recommended by European physicians for ailments of the colon and bowel. It was said to be an invaluable aid, moreover, in returning those undergoing fits to normality: brandy in at one end, and a few blows of dark shag at the other. The erotic potential of puffing fragrant tobacco into the bottom of one's beloved did not escape the public imagination: Fragonard, among others, represented the act on canvas. Reginald Whiff professes horror at the prospect; I have yet to encounter a devotee of the clyster. Can the modern world be so unimaginative?

Index

Recommended stockists

C Aston, Royal Exchange Shopping Centre, Exchange Street, Manchester, M2 7DB. Tel: 0161 832 7895.

James Barber, 33 Kirkgate, Otley, LS21 3HN. Tel: 01943 462603; fax: 01943 468770.

Benson & Hedges, 13 Old Bond Street, London W1. Tel: 0171 493 1825.

Birchalls of Blackpool, 14 Talbot Road, Blackpool FY1 1LG. Tel: 01253 24218.

E. Burkitt, 117 Church Road, Hove, Sussex. Tel: 01273 731351.

Churchills of Norwich, 32 St Andrew's Street, Norwich NR2 4AF. Tel: 01603 626437.

Dallings of Ayr, Burns Statue Square, Ayr KY7 1SU. Tel: 01292 265799.

Lewis Darbey & Co., 28-32 Wyndham Arcade, Mill Lane, Cardiff, CF1 1FJ. Tel: 01222 233443.

Davidoff, 35 St James's Street, London SW1A 1HD. Tel: 0171 930 3079.

Alfred Dunhill, 30 Duke Street, London SW1Y 6DL. Tel: 0171 499 6471.

J.J. Fox, 19 St James's Street, London SW1A 1ES. Tel: 0171 930 3787; fax: 0171 495 0097.

Gauntleys of Nottingham, 4 High Street, Nottingham NG1 2ET. Tel: 01159 417973.

Harrison & Simmonds of Bedford, 80 High Street, Bedford MK40 1NN. Tel and fax: 01234 266711.

Harrison & Simmonds of Cambridge, 17 St John's Street, Cambridge, CB2 1TW. Tel and fax: 01223 324515.

Harrods, Knightsbridge, London SW1X 9QF. Tel: 0171 730 1234; fax: 0171 581 9590.

Havana Club, 165 Sloane Street, London SW1X 7XL; fax: 0171 245 0895.

Jayems, 125 Victoria Street, London SW1E 5LA. Tel: 0171 828 1472.

John Hollingsworth & Son, 5 Temple Row, Birmingham B2 5LG. Tel: 0121 236 3696.

Lands, 29 Central Chambers, Henley Street, Stratford-upon-Avon CV37 6QN. Tel: 01789 292508.

Herbert Love, 31 Queensferry Street, Edinburgh EH2 4QU. Tel and fax: 0131 225 8082.

McGahey the Tobacconist, 245 High Street, Exeter EX4 3NZ. Tel: 01392 496111; fax: 01392 496113.

Sautter of Mayfair, 106 Mount Street, London W1Y 1AB. Tel and fax: 0171 499 4866.

The Segar and Snuff Parlour, 27a The Market, Covent Garden, London WC2. Tel: 0171 836 8345.

Selfridges, 400 Oxford Street, London W1A 1AB. Tel: 0171 629 1234; fax: 0171 491 1880.

Shervingtons of High Holborn, 337 High Holborn, London WC1V 7PX. Tel: 0171 405 2929; fax: 0171 803 8887.

G. Smith and Sons, 74 Charing Cross Road, London WC2. Tel: 0171 836 7422.

Tobacco House, 9 St Vincent Place, Glasgow G1 2DW. Tel and Fax: 0141 226 4586.

Tobacco World (Cheltenham), Unit F7, Regent Arcade, Cheltenham GL50 1JZ. Tel and fax: 01242 222037.

Tobacco World of Chester, 78 Northgate Street, Chester CH1 2HT. Tel and fax: 01244 348821.

Walter Thurgood, 161-162 Salisbury House, London Wall, London EC2M 5QD. Tel: 0171 628 5437; fax: 0171 930 5887.

Frederick Tranter, 5 Church Street, Abbey Green, Bath BA1 1NL. Tel and fax: 01225 466197.